M000159452

STUFF YOU CAN MAKE TO DECORATE
Your Windows

STUFF YOU CAN MAKE TO DECORATE
Your Furniture

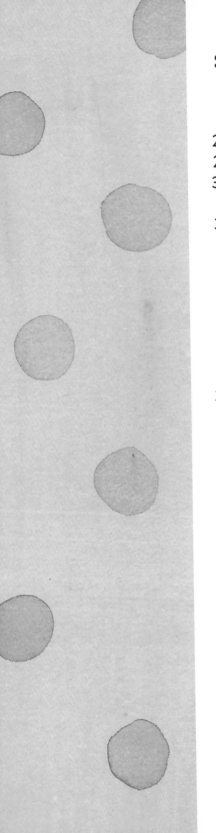

STUFF YOU CAN MAKE TO DECORATE

your Walls

STUFF YOU CAN MAKE TO DECORATE

your Bed

STUFF YOU CAN MAKE TO ORGANIZE

your Desk

STUFF YOU CAN MAKE TO ORGANIZE
your Closet

STUFF YOU CAN MAKE TO DECORATE
for the Holidays

Our mom decorates our house, but we decorate our rooms.

Our rooms are our special spaces. They are where we craft and create and make things and write and read and hope and dream.

Even though we are twins, we like to decorate in different ways. Westleigh is all about neutral colors, like blush and cream and white with gold accents. Her room has shiplap walls, hand-painted signs, pictures of her friends, and a faux fur blanket and pillows that say hello. Whitney is all about bright, happy colors, like yellow and blue and white. She has a sliding barn door between her closet and the bathroom. She has picture ledges full of beautiful artwork, baskets full of books, tons of green plants, and a tufted bench at the end of her bed that's full of blankets with her name on them.

Two girls, two rooms. Each special and amazing and wonderful and creative.

And that's why we wrote this book.

We wanted to give you ideas and projects and crafts and DIYs and design tips that you can use for your own room. We wanted to inspire you to follow your heart and decorate your space in *your own style*. We wanted to show you how to create a space that you will love.

A space you can call your own. A space you designed.
A space that's perfect. And unique. And special. And one of a kind.
Just. Like. You.
Happy decorating,

Whitney and Westleigh

At the beginning of each craft, you'll see one, two, or three paintbrushes. They show you how easy or difficult the craft is. You'll also see a clock...or maybe several clocks. These let you know how much time you can expect to spend completing the craft.

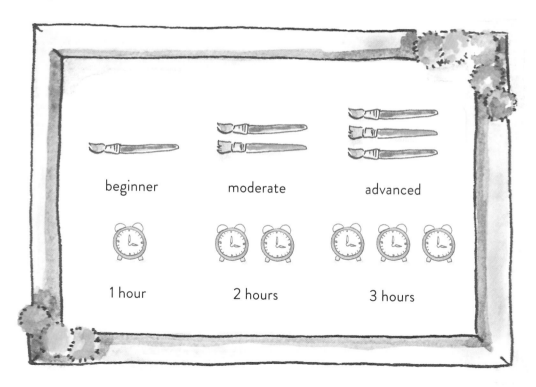

beginner   moderate   advanced

1 hour   2 hours   3 hours

STUFF YOU CAN MAKE TO DECORATE

Your Spaces

SWEATER VASE

SKILL LEVEL

TIME

SUPPLIES

- ☐ round glass vase 10 inches tall
- ☐ old sweater that matches your room
- ☐ painter's tape
- ☐ scissors
- ☐ fabric glue
- ☐ flowers
- ☐ ruler

INSTRUCTIONS

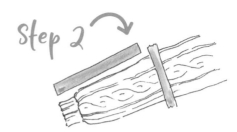

Step 2

1 Measure 12 inches up one sleeve of the sweater.

2 Mark it with painter's tape.

3 Cut a straight line on the sweater just below the painter's tape.

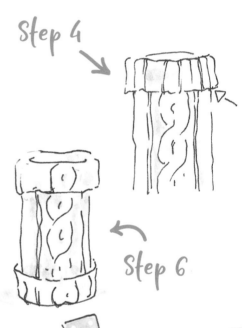

Step 4

4 Turn the detached sleeve inside out. Fold down 1 inch of one end.

5 Glue along the fold with fabric glue.

6 Repeat steps 4 and 5 with the other end of the sleeve.

7 Let the glue dry.

8 Turn the sleeve right-side out. Slide the sleeve onto the vase.

Step 6

9 Fill the vase with flowers.

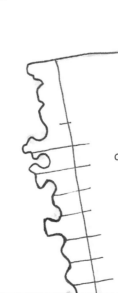

All done!

Westleigh says...

There are so many different color combinations of sweaters. Find one that works for your room.

Whitney says...

We like to make several vases with sweaters of different colors.

FLOWER-POWER GARLAND

SKILL LEVEL

TIME

SUPPLIES

- [ ] flower template (make your own by tracing ours on page 139 and cutting it out)
- [ ] leaf template (trace ours on page 142 and cut it out)
- [ ] 48 inches of leather cord
- [ ] 1 sheet of red felt (all the felt in this craft should be fairly thick)
- [ ] 1 sheet of blue felt
- [ ] 1 sheet of yellow felt
- [ ] 1 sheet of green felt
- [ ] 1 sheet of pink felt
- [ ] tiny hole punch
- [ ] scissors
- [ ] pencil

INSTRUCTIONS

1. Place your flower template on the red felt and trace around it with a pencil.

2. Trace as many flowers as you can fit on the felt page and cut them out.

3. Repeat steps 1 and 2 with the blue felt.

4. Repeat steps 1 and 2 with the yellow felt.

5. Repeat steps 1 and 2 with the pink felt.

6. Repeat steps 1 and 2 using the leaf template with the green felt.

7. Using the tiny hole punch, punch 2 holes in each flower and leaf as shown.

8. Thread a red flower onto the leather cord.

9. Thread a blue flower onto the leather cord, leaving 3 inches between each flower.

10. Keep threading the flowers and leaves, alternating colors, until you have filled up the entire leather cord.

Step 2

Step 7

Finished!

FLOWER HOOKS

SKILL LEVEL

TIME

SUPPLIES

- [ ] sticky-backed hooks with wood flower cutouts (you can find them at a craft store)
- [ ] large silk flowers
- [ ] glue
- [ ] scissors

INSTRUCTIONS

1. Remove the silk flowers from the stems.

2. Place a silk flower on the flower cutout at the top of a hook.

3. Glue the flower to the wood flower.

4. Let it dry.

5. Repeat steps 2 through 4 for as many hooks as you need.

6. Your flower hooks are ready to decorate your room with.

Step 1

Finito!

Westleigh says...

You can also paint a design around the edges of the hook before you glue the flower.

Whitney says...

I use these to organize my hair accessories. They are the perfect place for all my scrunchies.

EMBROIDERY-HOOP WELCOME SIGN

SKILL LEVEL

TIME

SUPPLIES

- ☐ WELCOME template (make your own by tracing ours on page 138, or create one on a computer and print it out)
- ☐ large embroidery hoop
- ☐ drop-cloth fabric
- ☐ paint marker
- ☐ scissors
- ☐ pencil
- ☐ six different types of silk flower blooms
- ☐ glue

Too cute!

INSTRUCTIONS

1. Open the embroidery hoop and separate the two hoops.

2. Place the larger hoop on the drop cloth fabric and draw a big circle around the hoop with about a 4-inch border.

3. Cut out the circle.

4. Place your WELCOME template under the drop cloth. You should be able to see the writing through the drop cloth.

5. Trace the word WELCOME with a pencil.

6. Use a paint marker to trace over your pencil lines.

7. Let it dry.

8. Place the smaller embroidery circle on a table.

9. Place the drop-cloth material with the word WELCOME on top of it.

10. Place the larger embroidery hoop on top and slide it into place.

11. Trim off any excess material.

12. Glue the silk flowers to the upper left of the back of the embroidery hoop.

13. Let it dry.

14. Your embroidery hoop is now ready to decorate with.

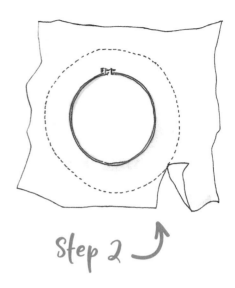

Step 2

Step 9

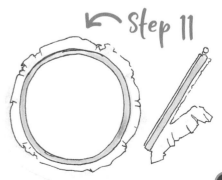

Step 11

5

SCRABBLE FAMILY ARTWORK

SKILL LEVEL

TIME

SUPPLIES

- ☐ 8 by 11-inch board from a craft store
- ☐ Scrabble tiles from a craft store
- ☐ wood glue
- ☐ picture hanger

Fun!

INSTRUCTIONS

1. Make a list of all the people in your family. (You can include your pets too.)

2. Find the letters that the names have in common.

3. Sketch a crossword puzzle on a piece of paper by combining the names at the same letter.

4. If the names don't share any letters, include the names of friends or extended family.

5. Once your puzzle is complete, find the Scrabble letters that match your sketch.

6. Use the Scrabble letters to lay out the puzzle on your piece of wood.

7. Glue the Scrabble pieces in place.

8. Add a picture hanger to the back.

9. Your family Scrabble artwork is ready to hang.

Step 5

FLOWER- BRANCH ARTWORK

SKILL LEVEL

TIME

SUPPLIES

- [ ] wood branch
- [ ] jute twine
- [ ] 12 different silk flowers
- [ ] scissors
- [ ] ruler

INSTRUCTIONS

1. Cut 12 pieces of jute twine 12 inches long.

2. Tie a piece of twine to the end of one flower stem. Use a double knot.

3. Repeat for the other 11 flowers.

4. Lay the branch horizontally on a table.

5. Tie each of the flowers to the branch so they hang down. Use a double knot each time.

6. Your flower-branch artwork is ready to hang on the wall.

Step 2

Step 5

looks great!

ANIMAL BOOKENDS

SKILL LEVEL

TIME

SUPPLIES

- [ ] 2 plastic animals
- [ ] 2 L-shaped bookends
- [ ] craft paint designed for plastic
- [ ] craft glue
- [ ] paintbrush
- [ ] pencil

Westleigh says...

My favorite color is pink. I love picking the color that matches my room.

Whitney says...

My favorite color is yellow. I think this would be a fun craft with flowers glued to the bookends too.

INSTRUCTIONS

1. Choose a paint color that matches your room.

2. Paint the animals with the craft paint.

3. Let them dry.

4. Paint a second coat.

5. Let it dry.

6. Place one of the animals in the corner of one L-shaped bookend.

7. Mark with a pencil where the animal attaches to the bookend.

8. Place a drop of glue on your pencil mark.

9. Place the animal on the glue.

10. Repeat steps 6 through 9 with the other bookend.

11. Let bookends dry.

12. You are ready to decorate.

Step 2

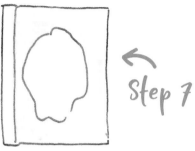

Step 7

Step 9

Finished!

PERSONALIZED WELCOME MAT

SKILL LEVEL

TIME

SUPPLIES

- ☐ plain jute welcome mat
- ☐ large chipboard letter
  (approximately 12 inches tall)
- ☐ black marker
- ☐ black craft paint
- ☐ small paintbrush

INSTRUCTIONS

1. Place the chipboard letter in the center of the welcome mat.

2. Trace around it with the marker.

3. Fill in the rest of the outline of the letter with the black craft paint.

4. Let it dry.

5. Paint another coat.

6. Let it dry.

7. Place your personalized mat in your room or just outside your door to welcome your guests.

Step 2

Step 3

STUFF YOU CAN MAKE TO DECORATE
Your Door

WELCOME

MONOGRAMMED WHITEBOARD

SKILL LEVEL

TIME

SUPPLIES

- [ ] small whiteboard
- [ ] alphabet stickers
- [ ] painter's tape
- [ ] ribbon
- [ ] scissors
- [ ] fabric glue

Westleigh says...

Ask a question on your message board, like "What is your favorite food?" It's fun to read all the answers.

Whitney says...

Most whiteboards come with a clip-on pen. Glue a flower to the top of the pen to make your whiteboard even cuter.

INSTRUCTIONS

1. Lay the whiteboard on a table.

2. Place a piece of painter's tape 2 inches from the bottom of the whiteboard. This will be a guide for your letters.

3. Find the alphabet stickers that spell out your name.

4. Find the middle letter of your name and line it up with the bottom of the tape.

5. Next, add the two letters on either side of the middle letter.

6. Keep adding stickers until you spell out your name. Make sure all the stickers are firmly attached.

7. Remove the tape.

8. Cut four pieces of ribbon for each side of the whiteboard.

9. Glue the ribbons to the whiteboard using fabric glue.

10. Let the glue dry.

11. Have a grown-up help you hang up your message board on the outside of your door.

12. Your message board is ready for your friends and family to leave you messages on.

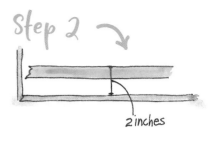

Step 2

2 inches

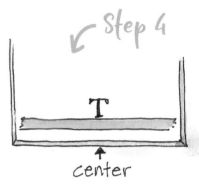

Step 4

T

center

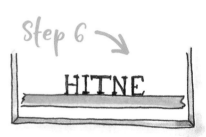

Step 6

HITNE

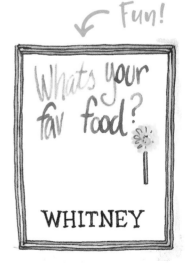

Fun!

Whats your fav food?

WHITNEY

WASHI-TAPE DOOR

SKILL LEVEL

TIME

SUPPLIES

- ☐ polka-dot washi tape
- ☐ striped washi tape
- ☐ patterned washi tape
- ☐ solid color washi tape
- ☐ scissors
- ☐ ruler

Too cute!

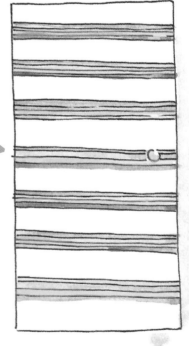

INSTRUCTIONS

1. Measure 6 inches down from the top of your door. You will be adding horizontal strips of washi tape in groups of 4.

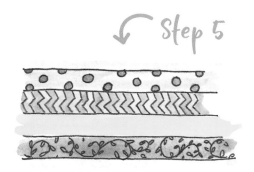

↙ Step 5

2. Add a horizontal stripe of polka-dot washi tape to your door.

3. Add a horizontal stripe of striped washi tape beneath the polka-dot washi tape.

4. Add a horizontal stripe of solid washi tape next to the other pieces of tape.

5. Add a horizontal stripe of patterned washi tape next to the other pieces of tape.

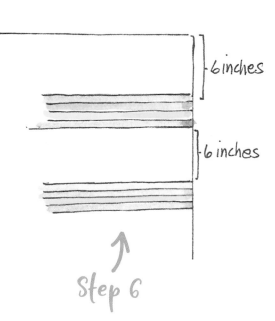

6 inches

6 inches

6. Measure another 6 inches down from the patterned washi tape.

7. Repeat steps 2 through 5.

8. Measure another 6 inches down from the lowest piece of patterned washi tape.

9. Repeat steps 2 through 5.

↑

Step 6

10. Make sure all the tape on your door is pressed down.

11. Your door is ready for guests.

YOU'VE GOT MAIL(BOX)

SKILL LEVEL

TIME

SUPPLIES

- [ ] unpainted wood mailbox (you can find one in the unfinished wood section of a craft store)
- [ ] white acrylic craft paint
- [ ] metal label holder (look in the scrapbook section of a craft store)
- [ ] scissors
- [ ] double-sided adhesive
- [ ] paintbrush
- [ ] card stock

Finished!

INSTRUCTIONS

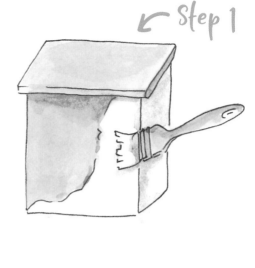

← Step 1

1. Paint the unfinished wood mailbox white.

2. Let it dry.

3. Paint a second coat on the mailbox.

4. Let it dry.

5. Using your home computer, print out the word MAIL on card stock.

6. Cut out the word MAIL and put it inside the metal label holder.

Step 6

MAIL

7. Attach the metal label to your mailbox with double-sided adhesive.

8. Have a grown-up help you attach it to the wall just outside your door.

9. Your mailbox is ready for mail.

Bonus idea ↘

Westleigh says...

You could also paint the mailbox a color that matches your room instead of white.

Whitney says...

I like to add polka dots to mine using the end of a pencil and coordinating craft paint.

33

TIED-ON RAG WREATH

SKILL LEVEL

TIME

SUPPLIES

- [ ] 18-inch embroidery hoop
- [ ] ½ yard of polka-dot fabric
- [ ] ½ yard of striped fabric
- [ ] ½ yard of patterned fabric
- [ ] scissors
- [ ] ruler

Westleigh says...

Instead of cutting the fabric, you can rip off a long piece 3 inches wide and cut it into 8-inch lengths.

Whitney says...

The edges of the material fray a little bit when you make this project. Don't worry about that. We think it makes it cuter.

INSTRUCTIONS

1. Cut the polka-dot fabric into 25 strips. Make all the strips for this project about 8 inches long and 3 inches wide.

Step 1

2. Cut the striped fabric into 25 strips.

3. Cut the patterned fabric into 25 strips.

4. Tie the end of one strip of polka-dot fabric to the embroidery hoop and let the rest of the strip hang down.

5. Repeat step 4 with a strip of striped fabric.

6. Repeat step 4 with a strip of patterned fabric.

Step 7

7. Continue working around the embroidery hoop until it is completely covered with knotted pieces of fabric.

8. Trim off excess fabric to make sure the wreath is even.

9. Fluff the wreath and hang it on your door.

looks great!

WELCOME WHITEBOARD

SKILL LEVEL

TIME

SUPPLIES

- [ ] small whiteboard
- [ ] alphabet stickers
- [ ] sticky Velcro tape
- [ ] ribbon
- [ ] scissors
- [ ] fabric glue
- [ ] silk flowers
- [ ] dry erase marker
- [ ] Scrabble tile holder

Perfect!

INSTRUCTIONS

1. Glue a piece of ribbon around the edge of the whiteboard.

2. Let it dry.

3. Glue a Scrabble tile holder to the front of the whiteboard.

4. Let it dry.

5. Cut a small square of Velcro tape.

6. Peel the backing off one side of the Velcro tape and stick it to the Scrabble tile holder.

7. Peel the backing off the other side of the Velcro tape and stick it to the dry erase marker.

8. Attach your dry erase marker to the Scrabble tile holder with the Velcro tape.

9. Find the letters to spell Welcome in the alphabet stickers and stick them to the top center of the whiteboard. Decorate corners with silk flowers using fabric glue.

10. Your welcome whiteboard is ready for your door.

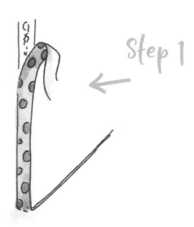

Step 1

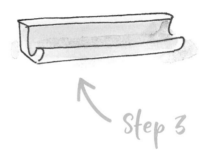

Step 3

WELCOME

Step 9

COLORFUL PICTURE RIBBONS

SKILL LEVEL

TIME

SUPPLIES

- [ ] 2 rolls of ribbon
- [ ] mini clothespins
- [ ] pictures
- [ ] 4 brass rings (you can find these in the sewing section of a craft store)
- [ ] fabric glue
- [ ] scissors
- [ ] sticky-backed hooks (we use Command brand)
- [ ] ruler

Westleigh says...
You can also glue a flower onto the top of the ribbons just below the brass rings.

Whitney says...
I clip notes from my friends and drawings to the ribbons too.

INSTRUCTIONS

1. Cut four 36-inch pieces of ribbon.

2. Wrap the end of a piece of ribbon around the edge of a brass ring.

3. Use fabric glue to hold the ribbon in place.

4. Repeat steps 2 and 3 to attach the other 3 pieces of ribbon to the other 3 brass rings.

5. Let them dry.

6. Fold the other end of the ribbons and cut them in a triangle to make a decorative end.

7. Clip the clothespins onto the ribbons about every 6 inches.

8. Stick 4 hooks across the top of your door about 5 inches apart.

9. Hang a brass ring on each of the hooks.

10. Use the clothespins to clip photos of your friends to the ribbons.

Step 2
↓

Step 6
↑

Finito! ↱

CHALKBOARD MESSAGE BOARD

SKILL LEVEL

TIME

SUPPLIES

- [ ] 8 by 10-inch white craft canvas
- [ ] chalkboard paint
- [ ] paintbrush
- [ ] polka-dot ribbon
- [ ] glue
- [ ] chalk
- [ ] small canvas bag (you can find these in the scrapbook section of a craft store)
- [ ] sticky-backed hook (we use Command brand)
- [ ] scissors

INSTRUCTIONS

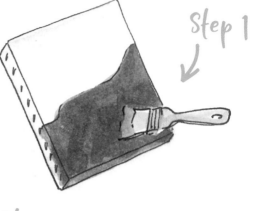

Step 1

1. Apply a coat of chalkboard paint to the canvas.

2. Let it dry.

3. Apply a second coat of chalkboard paint to the canvas.

4. Let it dry.

Step 5

5. Glue a polka-dot ribbon around the edge of the canvas.

6. Stick the hook to the top-right corner of your canvas.

7. Prime the painted canvas by rubbing the edge of a piece of chalk all over it. Wipe off the excess chalk. Your chalkboard is ready for writing.

Step 7

8. Put pieces of chalk in the canvas bag and hang it on the hook.

9. Have a grown-up help you hang your message board on your door. You're ready to share notes with friends!

All done!

OPEN/CLOSED DOOR HANGER

SKILL LEVEL

TIME

SUPPLIES

- ☐ unpainted wood door hanger
- ☐ white acrylic craft paint
- ☐ printouts of the words OPEN and CLOSED to fit on the door hanger
- ☐ pencil
- ☐ carbon paper
- ☐ colored paint markers

Beautiful! →

INSTRUCTIONS

1. Paint the front and sides of the door hanger white.

2. Let it dry.

3. Flip the door hanger over and paint the back.

4. Let it dry.

5. Place a piece of carbon paper with the shiny side down on top of the painted door hanger.

6. Place the printout of the word OPEN on top.

7. Trace the word OPEN with a pencil. Lift up the edge to make sure the word is being transferred onto the wood block.

8. Remove the printout and the carbon paper. The word OPEN should be traced in pencil on the block.

9. Use the paint markers to trace the word on the door hanger.

10. Let the paint dry.

11. Repeat steps 5 through 10 with the word CLOSED on the other side.

12. Your door hanger is ready.

Step 1 →

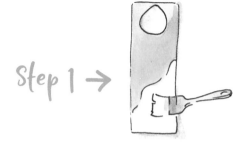

Step 7

Step 9

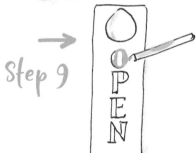

Westleigh says...
If you don't want to paint the letters, you could just add alphabet stickers instead.

Whitney says...
I like to add glitter flower stickers to my door hanger after I've painted it.

17

Design Tip:

HOW TO CHOOSE A THEME FOR YOUR ROOM

Whitney and Westleigh say...

Sometimes decorating your room is easier when you have a theme. The theme can be based on lots of different things, like a color pattern, your favorite movie, or your favorite thing to do. Choosing a theme for your room is so much easier than you might think. We always start with some of our favorite things and go from there. If you need help figuring out a decorating theme for your room, try these tips:

1 Think of your favorite color and a color that matches it. Write them down.

....

....

....

2 Think of your favorite thing to do. It could be your favorite game to play with friends, or your favorite sport, or your favorite thing to do when you have a few minutes. Write it down.

....

....

....

3 Think of your favorite book or movie. Write it down.

....

....

....

Now look at the list you have written. Chances are, you have a great place to start for themes for your room.

You can also combine different things on your list to create a decorating theme that shows off your uniqueness and your personality.

That's the theme that will be perfect for your room. It's special and wonderful and one of a kind.

Just like you.

STUFF YOU CAN MAKE TO DECORATE YOUR

Windows

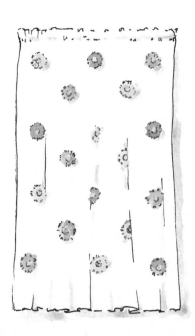

18

FLOWER-POWER SHEERS

SKILL LEVEL

TIME

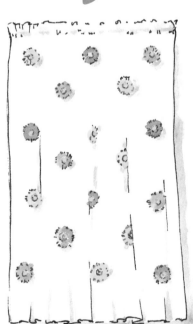

Voilà!

SUPPLIES

- [ ] set of sheer curtains
- [ ] 36 silk flowers
  (Gerbera daisies
  work best)

- [ ] drop cloth
- [ ] scissors
- [ ] fabric glue

INSTRUCTIONS

1. Cut the stems off the flowers (sometimes you can just pull them right off). Remove any backing. We will be using only the flower petals for this craft.

2. Lay a drop cloth or some plastic on the floor to protect your surface from the glue.

Step 1

3. Lay the curtain on the drop cloth or plastic.

4. Lay 18 flowers on each sheer—3 across the top, then a row of 2, another row of 3, a row of 2, a row of 3, a row of 2, and a row of 3. There should be 7 rows of flowers in all.

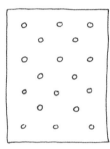
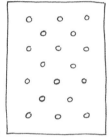

Step 4

5. After all the flowers are laid out and you are happy with your pattern, use the fabric glue to glue all the flowers in place.

6. Let the glue dry.

7. Your flower sheers are ready to hang.

Westleigh says...

Did you know that sheer curtains come in different colors? Choose a color that matches your room.

Whitney says...

I use painter's tape to hold the flowers in place as they are drying.

19

STRIPED CURTAIN RODS

SKILL LEVEL

TIME

SUPPLIES

- [ ] wood dowel 34 inches longer than your window
- [ ] 2 curtain rod finials
- [ ] 2 curtain rod brackets
- [ ] pink acrylic craft paint
- [ ] paintbrush
- [ ] painter's tape

Finished!

INSTRUCTIONS

1. Wrap 4-inch pieces of painter's tape around the dowel, side by side, until the entire dowel is covered.

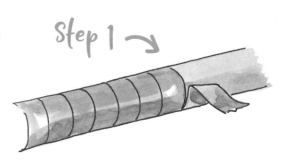

Step 1 ⤳

2. After the dowel rod is covered, leave the first piece of wrapped painter's tape. Remove the second. Leave the third. Remove the fourth. Continue until you've removed every other piece of painter's tape.

3. Using a paintbrush and craft paint, paint the exposed wood on the dowel.

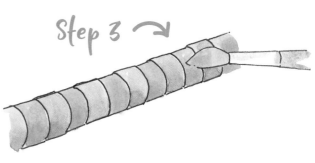

Step 3 ⤳

4. Let it dry.

5. Paint a second coat.

6. Let it dry.

7. Peel off the rest of the painter's tape and throw it away.

8. Have a grown-up help you add the finials and hang up the curtains.

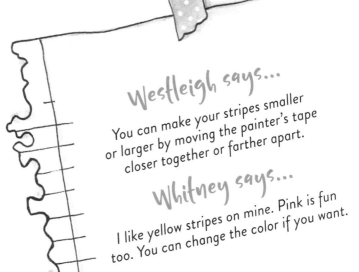

Westleigh says...

You can make your stripes smaller or larger by moving the painter's tape closer together or farther apart.

Whitney says...

I like yellow stripes on mine. Pink is fun too. You can change the color if you want.

20

POM-POM TRIMMED CURTAINS

SKILL LEVEL

TIME

SUPPLIES

- ☐ set of white curtain panels
- ☐ package of multicolored pom-poms (you can find these at a craft store)
- ☐ fabric glue
- ☐ scissors
- ☐ ruler

INSTRUCTIONS

1. Lay a drop cloth or some plastic on the floor to protect your surface from the glue.

2. Lay the curtain flat on the floor.

3. Place pom-poms along the inner edge of the curtain 2 inches apart.

4. After the pom-poms are laid out and you are happy with your pattern, use the fabric glue to glue the pom-poms in place.

5. Keep gluing until all the pom-poms are glued down to the edge of the curtain.

6. Let the glue dry.

7. Repeat steps 2 through 6 for the second panel.

8. Your pom-pom curtains are ready to hang.

Awesome!

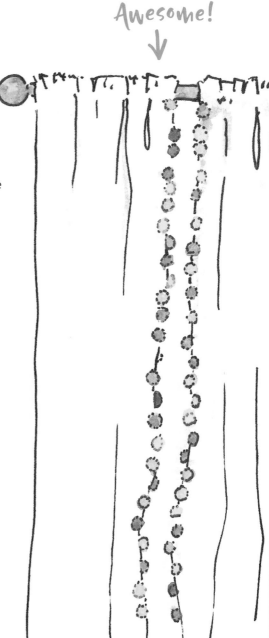

Step 4

21

POM-POM TIEBACKS

SKILL LEVEL

TIME

SUPPLIES

- [ ] yarn that is color-coordinated with your room
- [ ] 5-inch-square piece of cardboard
- [ ] ribbon
- [ ] scissors
- [ ] fabric glue
- [ ] ruler

Westleigh says...

Instead of gluing the pom-pom to the end of the ribbon, you can glue it about 3 inches from the end and let the rest of the ribbon hang.

Whitney says...

You could also braid a set of ribbons together instead of just using one.

INSTRUCTIONS

1. We are all about pom-poms here and use them for so many different crafts. See the tutorial on page 130 to learn how to make pom-poms.

2. Using the 5-inch piece of cardboard, make 2 large pom-poms for each tieback.

3. Fluff and trim your pom-poms until they are round.

4. Cut a 12-inch piece of ribbon.

5. Lay the ribbon flat.

6. Glue 1 large pom-pom to each end of the ribbon.

7. Let it dry.

8. Repeat steps 4 through 7 for the other curtain tieback.

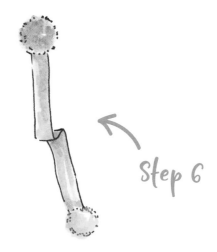

Step 6

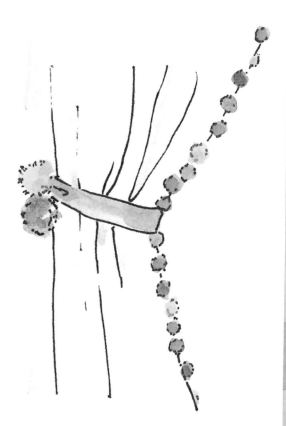

22

Design Tip:

HOW TO CHOOSE YOUR FAVORITE PATTERN

Whitney and Westleigh say...

Finding a fun pattern for your room is one way to show your personality. Whether it's stripes or zebra print or polka dots or zigzags, picking a pattern for your room is so much easier than you think. We always start by talking with our mom and letting her know our ideas and what we want our room to look like. And then? We start with our favorite. If you need help choosing your favorite pattern (or patterns), maybe these tips will get you started:

1. With a pen and paper, start drawing doodles. Keep drawing until you have covered most of the paper. What did you draw the most of? Was it stripes? Or hearts? Or arrows? Write it down.

2. Have your mom take you to the fabric store. Walk through the aisles. Is there a pattern that makes you happy? Write it down.

3. Stop by the scrapbook section of a craft store. Look through all the paper. Is there a pattern there that works for you? Write it down.

Now look at your list of patterns. Do you see a common pattern? That's the one that works in your room.

It's amazing...

Just like you.

STUFF YOU CAN MAKE TO DECORATE YOUR

Furniture

23

CRACKLE-GLUE TABLETOP

SKILL LEVEL

TIME

SUPPLIES

- ☐ small wood table
- ☐ pink latex paint
- ☐ white latex paint
- ☐ Elmer's Glue
- ☐ painter's tape
- ☐ paintbrush
- ☐ drop cloth

Westleigh says...

There are so many different color combinations that work well with this project. I like to paint a table with gold and white.

Whitney says...

This project also works well with the top of a stool.

INSTRUCTIONS

Step 3

Step 5

Step 7

Step 8

1. Place the table on a drop cloth or large piece of plastic. Make sure your table is clean and you've wiped down the top to remove any dirt.

2. Leave the tabletop exposed but mask the rest of the table with painter's tape.

3. Paint the tabletop pink. This is the color you want to show through the crackle.

4. Let it dry.

5. Brush Elmer's Glue onto the tabletop over the pink paint.

6. Let the glue dry slightly until it is tacky. Don't let the glue dry all the way or the crackle won't work.

7. When the glue is tacky, brush on a coat of white paint. Brush the paint only in one direction. Keep brushing in one direction until the entire tabletop is covered.

8. Step back and watch the white paint pull away and "crackle," letting the pink paint show through.

9. Let the paint dry.

10. Brush a final thin coat of Elmer's Glue to seal in the crackle.

11. Let dry.

Done! →

24

WHAT'S YOUR NAME? CHAIR

SKILL LEVEL

TIME

SUPPLIES

- [ ] wood chair
- [ ] raised sticker alphabet
- [ ] primer
- [ ] white latex paint
- [ ] drop cloth

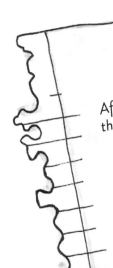

Westleigh says...

After the chair is dry, you can go over the letters with a paint pen if you want them to stand out more.

Whitney says...

We like to add pillows to our chairs. There are some fun pillow projects on pages 86 and 90.

INSTRUCTIONS

1. Place the chair on a drop cloth or large piece of plastic. Make sure your chair is clean and you've wiped it down to remove any dirt.

2. Find the stickers that spell out your name.

3. Remove them and stick them on the top of the back of the chair.

4. Paint the chair (including the stickers) with a coat of primer.

5. Let it dry.

6. Paint a coat of white latex paint over the primer.

7. Let it dry.

8. Paint a second coat of white paint.

9. Let the last coat dry.

10. Your personal chair is ready for your room.

Step 4

Looks great!

25

CHECKERBOARD TABLE

SKILL LEVEL

TIME

(plus drying time)

SUPPLIES

- ☐ small wood table
- ☐ white latex paint
- ☐ black latex paint
- ☐ ruler
- ☐ pencil
- ☐ painter's tape
- ☐ paintbrush
- ☐ drop cloth
- ☐ checkers

Cool!

INSTRUCTIONS

1. Place the table on a drop cloth or large piece of plastic. Make sure your table is clean and you've wiped down the top to remove any dirt.

2. Tape off a 24 by 24-inch square in the center of the table.

3. Paint the square with two coats of white latex paint. Let the square dry each time.

4. Make a pencil mark on the painter's tape every 3 inches across the top and bottom of the square.

5. Repeat the same process with both sides of the square. You should now have 8 vertical (up and down) columns and 8 horizontal (side to side) rows.

6. Mask every other vertical column with painter's tape.

7. Mask every other horizontal row with painter's tape.

8. Paint the exposed squares with two coats of black latex paint. Let the squares dry each time.

9. Carefully remove the painter's tape and throw it away.

10. Now mask the vertical columns you didn't mask the first time.

11. Mask the horizontal rows you didn't mask the first time.

12. Paint the exposed squares with two coats of black paint. Let the squares dry each time.

13. Carefully remove the painter's tape and throw it away.

14. Your checkerboard is ready to play—just add checkers.

Step 3

Step 6

Step 8

26

WRAPPING- PAPER BOOKCASE

SKILL LEVEL

TIME

SUPPLIES

- [ ] small bookcase
- [ ] wrapping paper
- [ ] double-sided tape
- [ ] ruler
- [ ] scissors
- [ ] pencil

INSTRUCTIONS

1 Remove everything from the bookcase and wipe it down to make sure it's ready for this project.

2 Use the ruler to measure the height and width of the back of one of your shelves.

3 On the back of the wrapping paper, draw a rectangle as high and wide as the back of the shelf.

4 Cut out the rectangle.

5 Stick pieces of double-sided tape around the edges of the back of the wrapping paper.

6 Press the wrapping paper in place on the back of the bookshelf.

7 Repeat steps 2 through 6 with each of the other shelves.

8 Your bookcase is ready to decorate.

Step 4 ➘

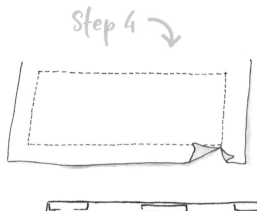

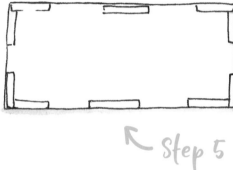

↖ Step 5

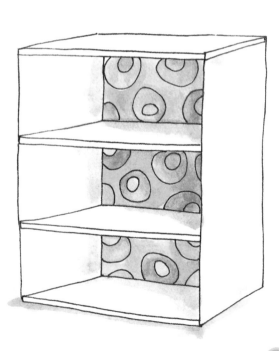

Done!

27

FLOWER STOOL

SKILL LEVEL

TIME

SUPPLIES

- ☐ wood stool
- ☐ flower template (make your own by tracing ours on page 139 and cutting it out)
- ☐ drop cloth
- ☐ white latex paint
- ☐ carbon paper
- ☐ pencil
- ☐ paint markers

INSTRUCTIONS

Step 2

1. Place the stool on a drop cloth or large piece of plastic. Make sure your stool is clean and you've wiped it down to remove any dirt.

2. Paint the stool with white paint and let it dry.

3. Apply a second coat and let it dry.

Step 6

4. Place a piece of carbon paper with the shiny side down on the top of the stool.

5. Place the flower template on top of the carbon paper.

6. Trace the outline of the flower with a pencil. Lift up the edge to make sure the flower is being transferred onto the top of the stool.

7. Remove the flower template and the carbon paper. The flower should now be traced in pencil on the stool.

8. Use the paint markers to fill in the flower on top of the stool.

9. Let the paint markers dry.

10. Your stool is ready to decorate your room with.

Step 8

69

STUFF YOU CAN MAKE TO DECORATE YOUR

Walls

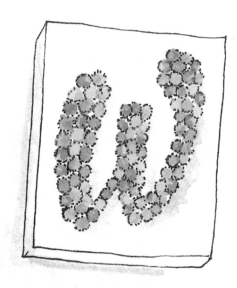

28

PICTURE-FRAME FLOWER WREATH

SKILL LEVEL

TIME

SUPPLIES

- [ ] small wood picture frame
- [ ] silk flowers in a variety of styles and sizes
- [ ] scissors
- [ ] painter's tape
- [ ] glue
- [ ] ribbon

Westleigh says...

One fun idea for this craft is to glue the flowers only to two adjoining sides of the frame, creating an asymmetrical picture-frame flower wreath.

Whitney says...

I use painter's tape to hold the flowers in place as they are drying.

INSTRUCTIONS

1. Remove the glass and backing from the picture frame. We will use only the picture frame for this craft.

2. Lay a drop cloth or some plastic on a tabletop to protect your surface from the glue.

3. Lay the picture frame on the drop cloth.

4. Cut the flowers off the ends of the stems. Remove any backing. We will use only the flower petals for this craft.

5. Glue the largest flower to the corner of the picture frame.

6. Lay out a pattern of large, medium, and small flowers around the edges of the frame. Glue the flowers in place as you go.

7. Keep gluing until the flowers completely cover the picture frame.

8. Let the glue dry.

9. Wrap a ribbon through the center of the top of the picture frame and hang it up.

Step 5

Step 6

Pretty!

29

BEST FRIEND HAND-PAINTED BLOCKS

SKILL LEVEL

TIME

SUPPLIES

- ☐ 2 wood blocks (you can find these at any craft store)
- ☐ white acrylic craft paint
- ☐ a computer printout of your name
- ☐ a computer printout of your best friend's name
- ☐ carbon paper
- ☐ pencil
- ☐ paint markers

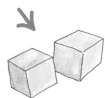

Too cute!

Amy

Westleigh

INSTRUCTIONS

1. Start by painting the tops and sides of both wood blocks white. Let them dry.

2. Flip the blocks over and paint the backs. Let them dry.

3. Place a piece of carbon paper with the shiny side down on top of a painted wood block.

4. Place the piece of paper with your name printed on it on top.

5. Trace your name with a pencil. Lift up the edge to make sure your name is being transferred onto the wood block.

6. Remove the printout and the carbon paper. Your name should be traced in pencil on the block.

7. Use the paint markers to trace your name on the block.

8. Let the paint dry.

9. Repeat steps 3 through 8 to make a matching block for your best friend.

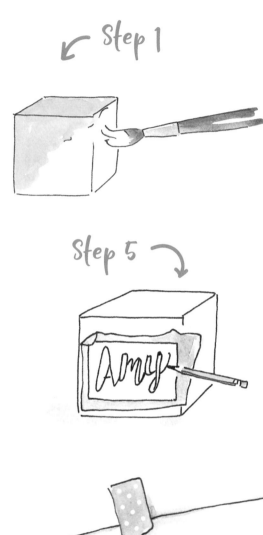

Step 1

Step 5

Westleigh says...

You can decorate your blocks with flowers or polka dots using the paint markers. Polka dots are my favorite.

Whitney says...

You could also add your favorite Scripture to your block.

30

FRAMED SCRIPTURE QUOTE

SKILL LEVEL

TIME

SUPPLIES

- ☐ favorite Scripture
- ☐ card stock
- ☐ floating frame (you can find these at craft stores)
- ☐ scissors

INSTRUCTIONS

1. Using your favorite computer font, print out your favorite Scripture on card stock.

2. A floating frame consists of two clear pieces of plastic held together by a frame. A small piece of rubber holds the frame together. Remove the piece of rubber and open the floating frame.

3. Place your Scripture verse in the center of one of the pieces of plastic. Place the other piece of plastic on top.

4. Replace the frame.

5. Your framed Scripture quote is ready to hang.

"Let your light shine for all to see."

Fantastic!

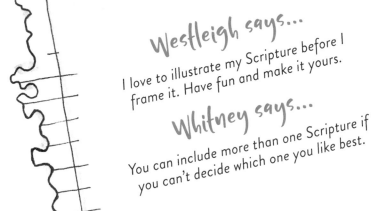

Westleigh says...
I love to illustrate my Scripture before I frame it. Have fun and make it yours.

Whitney says...
You can include more than one Scripture if you can't decide which one you like best.

31

POM-POM LETTER

SKILL LEVEL

TIME

SUPPLIES

- ☐ mini pom-poms of different colors (you can find bags of them in craft stores)
- ☐ 8 by 10-inch white canvas
- ☐ fabric glue
- ☐ pencil
- ☐ large computer printout of your monogram
- ☐ scissors

Westleigh says...

You can also glue a ribbon around the edge of the canvas if you want to add more color.

Whitney says...

You could hang up the art by a pom-pom string from the fabric store too.

INSTRUCTIONS

1. Cut out the monogram from the printout.

2. Center the letter on the canvas and trace around it with your pencil.

3. Remove the monogram from the canvas. You should now have an outline of your monogram.

4. Add a dot of fabric glue to one mini pom-pom.

5. Place the pom-pom on the canvas inside the pencil line.

6. Press in place.

7. Glue a second pom-pom onto the canvas. Press in place.

8. Alternate colors and keep gluing pom-poms until you have completely filled in the letter.

9. Let pom-poms dry before you hang up the art.

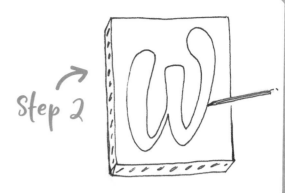

Step 2

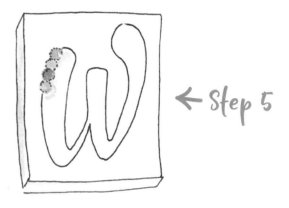

← Step 5

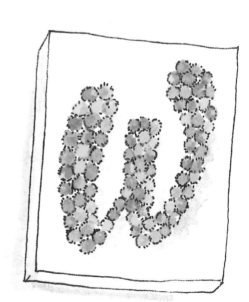

Finished!

32

Design Tip:

HOW TO CHOOSE A COLOR FOR YOUR ROOM

Whitney and Westleigh say...

Picking a color (or colors) for your room is so much easier than you think. We always start by talking with our mom and letting her know our ideas and what we want our room to look like. And then? We start with our favorite. Here are some tips that can help you figure out what your favorite colors are.

1 Close your eyes and think of a color. What color pops into your head right away? Write that color down.

. . . .

. . . .

. . . .

2 Look at your closet. What is your favorite outfit? What color is it? Write that color down.

. . . .

. . . .

. . . .

3 Open a box of crayons. What color do you reach for first? Write that color down.

. . . .

. . . .

. . . .

4 What color do you like to use when you draw? Write that color down.

. . . .

. . . .

. . . .

Now look at your list of colors. These are your favorites.
And those colors? They are perfect.
Just like you.

STUFF YOU CAN MAKE
TO DECORATE

Your Bed

33

"HELLO, FRIEND" DOTTED PILLOW COVER

SKILL LEVEL

TIME

SUPPLIES

- ☐ "Hello, friend" template (make your own by tracing ours on page 136, or create one on a computer and print it out)
- ☐ white pillow cover with a zipper (we get ours from IKEA)
- ☐ pink latex fabric paint
- ☐ yellow fabric paint
- ☐ pencil
- ☐ 2 foam circle stampers (you can find them in the paint section of a craft store)
- ☐ scissors
- ☐ 2 paper plates

INSTRUCTIONS

1. Place your "Hello, friend" template inside the pillow cover. You should be able to see the writing through the pillow cover.

2. Trace the words onto the pillow cover with a pencil.

3. Pour some pink latex paint onto a paper plate.

4. Pour some yellow latex paint onto another paper plate.

5. Use 1 foam circle stamper for each color.

6. Stamp a pink dot on the bottom of the "H" in "Hello."

7. Stamp a yellow dot just above the pink dot.

8. Keep stamping with alternating colors until you have covered all the pencil lines.

9. Let it dry.

10. Your pillow is ready to stuff.

Step 3
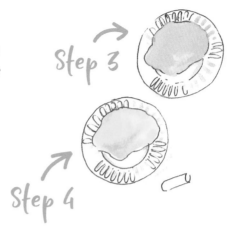

Step 4

Step 6

Done! →

34

JEAN POCKET PILLOW

SKILL LEVEL

TIME

SUPPLIES

- [ ] old pair of jeans
- [ ] white pillow
- [ ] fabric glue
- [ ] scissors
- [ ] pencil

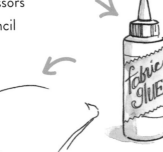

Westleigh says...
I like to add my favorite Scripture to my pillow too.

Whitney says...
I love to write on Post-it notes. You can put those in the pillow pocket too.

INSTRUCTIONS

1. Cut a back pocket out of the jeans. Trim around the jean pocket to prevent fraying.

2. Add fabric glue to the edges of the back of the pocket and glue it to the center of the pillow.

3. Let the fabric glue dry.

4. You now have the perfect place to keep a small notebook or diary.

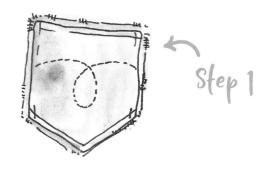

Step 1

Step 2

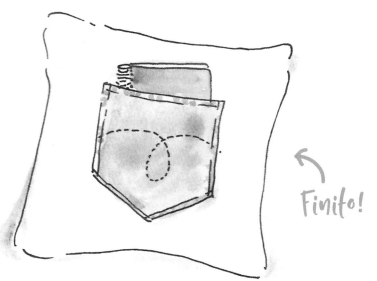

Finito!

35

POM-POM THROW

SKILL LEVEL

TIME

SUPPLIES

- [ ] store-bought throw with a loose weave
- [ ] yarn
- [ ] 5-inch square piece of cardboard

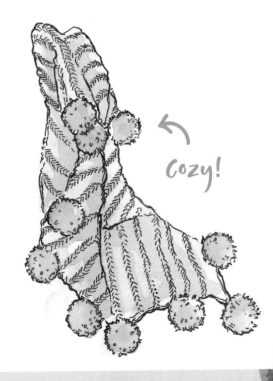

cozy!

INSTRUCTIONS

1. Choose a yarn color that goes well with the color of the store-bought blanket you will be using for this project.

2. We are all about pom-poms here and use them for so many different crafts. Follow the instructions on page 130 to make approximately 29 large pom-poms using a 5-inch piece of cardboard.

3. When making the pom-poms, make sure to leave extra yarn when you tie off the pom-pom in the middle.

4. When you've made all the pom-poms, lay the throw flat on the floor. Pull the weave slightly apart at one corner. Tie the strings of a pom-pom onto the corner of the throw.

5. Repeat for each of the other corners of the throw.

6. Place 5 pom-poms on 1 side of the throw to make sure they are evenly spaced. Don't tie them yet.

7. Once you are happy with the spacing, pull the weave slightly apart and tie the pom-poms to the throw.

8. Repeat with each of the other 3 sides. Your throw is ready—toss it on the bed or over a chair in your room!

Step 4

Step 5

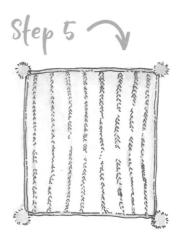

Step 7

36

T-SHIRT PILLOW

SKILL LEVEL

TIME

SUPPLIES

- ☐ T-shirt you don't wear but want to keep
- ☐ fabric pencil
- ☐ rectangular pillow form that fits inside your T-shirt
- ☐ scissors
- ☐ ruler

INSTRUCTIONS

1. Center the pillow inside the T-shirt.

2. Draw lines on the T-shirt 5 inches above the pillow and 5 inches below it.

3. Cut along your marks.

4. Cut strips 2 inches wide and 4 inches long in the top and bottom of the T-shirt square you have cut out.

5. Starting at the bottom, tie the first strip of the front of the T-shirt and the first strip of the back of the T-shirt together in a knot. Repeat with the second pair of strips. Continue tying until you have tied all the bottom strips together.

6. Repeat step 5 with the top.

7. Trim the ends of the knots so they are even.

8. Fluff the pillow and add it to your bed.

Step 2

Step 4

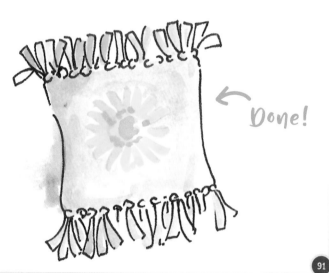

Done!

37

Design Tip:

HOW TO CHOOSE YOUR BEDDING

Whitney and Westleigh say...

When you're creating a design for your room, one of the best places to start is with the bedding. You can pick polka dots or stripes or a chevron or flowers for your bedding. We like to mix a lot of different patterns. We have a conversation with our mom and tell her our favorite patterns for our room. Then we look through print catalogs and online to find a design we like. Here are some of our favorite tips for picking out bedding for your room.

1 Start with a catalog from your favorite store. It's a great place to get inspiration even if you don't order the exact set from that store. Talk through your favorites with your mom. Write down your ideas.

2 Layering different patterns is one of the easiest ways to save money on the bedding for your room. Start with a solid color you like. Pick two other patterns that you can use to layer in the room.

3 If you don't want to order completely new bedding for your room, change out the pillows or a blanket draped over the end of the bed to create a fresh look.

Get creative. Layer patterns to create a unique look.
Add pillows and a throw blanket to change it up a bit.
This is your space. It's one-of-a-kind...
Just like you.

STUFF YOU CAN MAKE TO ORGANIZE
Your Desk

38

PAPER-TOWEL PENCIL HOLDERS

SKILL LEVEL

TIME

SUPPLIES

- ☐ 4 empty paper towel rolls
- ☐ washi tape
- ☐ 12 by 12-inch piece of cardboard
- ☐ white craft paint
- ☐ paintbrush
- ☐ scissors
- ☐ ruler
- ☐ pencil

Westleigh says...
You can use other colors of craft paint to decorate your organizer too.

Whitney says...
Add your name to the front of the organizer with stickers.

INSTRUCTIONS

1. Measure halfway up one empty paper towel roll and mark it with a pencil.

2. Cut the paper towel roll in half.

3. Repeat steps 1 and 2 with the other three paper towel rolls.

4. Paint the paper towel rolls and cardboard with white craft paint and let them dry.

5. Paint a second coat and let it dry.

6. Group the 8 half-rolls together in 2 rows of 4.

7. Start at one end and wrap the washi tape around the middle of the paper towel rolls.

8. Continue wrapping the paper towel rolls until they are sturdy and held in place.

9. Place the wrapped paper towel rolls onto the cardboard. Add mini pieces of washi tape at the bottom to hold them in place.

10. Fill the rolls with pencils, pens, and other office supplies.

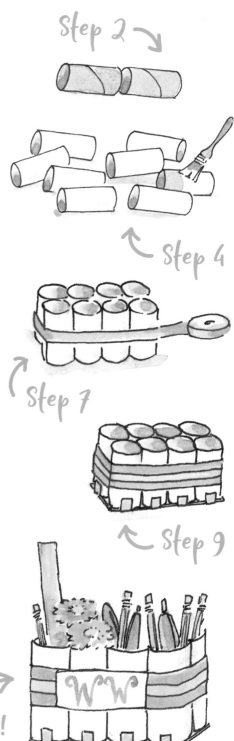

step 2

Step 4

Step 7

Step 9

looks great!

39

RIBBON PENCIL HOLDER

SKILL LEVEL

TIME

SUPPLIES

- [ ] plain pencil holder from a discount variety store
- [ ] craft glue
- [ ] three different types of patterned ribbon
- [ ] scissors
- [ ] Mod Podge
- [ ] paintbrush

Too cute!

INSTRUCTIONS

Step 2

1. Cut a piece of ribbon that wraps completely around your pencil holder and 1 inch farther.

2. Wrap the ribbon around the top of the pencil holder and glue it in place.

3. Add a piece of ribbon with a different pattern below the first ribbon. Glue the second piece of ribbon in place.

Step 6

4. Continue alternating ribbon pieces until you have completely covered the pencil holder.

5. Let it dry.

6. Turn to page 134 to learn how to use Mod Podge. Brush Mod Podge on the entire outside of the pencil holder.

7. Let it dry.

8. Your pencil holder is ready to hold pencils on your desk.

Westleigh says...

I made an extra pencil holder to keep in my locker.

Whitney says...

I like ribbon with smiley faces. It makes me happy.

40

NUMBERED DESK CALENDAR

SKILL LEVEL

TIME

SUPPLIES

- ☐ mini clipboard
- ☐ 2 sticky-backed hooks (we use Command brand)
- ☐ white tags from the craft store
- ☐ number stickers
- ☐ alphabet stickers
- ☐ large hole punch
- ☐ scissors

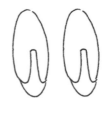

INSTRUCTIONS

1. Start by creating the month tags. Use the alphabet stickers to add each of these to a tag: Jan, Feb, Mar, Apr, May, June, July, Aug, Sept, Oct, Nov, Dec.

2. Next, use the number stickers to make tags for the numbers 1 through 31.

3. Stick the two hooks to the front of the clipboard side by side about 4 inches apart.

4. Put the month tags on the left hook and the date tags on the right hook.

5. Hang up your clipboard, and your calendar is ready.

6. Change the date tags for each day of the month and the month tags for each month of the year.

Step 1

Step 2

Done!

41

CEREAL-BOX DRAWER ORGANIZERS

SKILL LEVEL

TIME

SUPPLIES

- ☐ 5 empty cereal boxes
- ☐ contact paper that matches your room
- ☐ pencil
- ☐ scissors
- ☐ ruler

INSTRUCTIONS

1. Remove the plastic bags from inside the cereal boxes and make sure the boxes are clean.

2. Measure 4 inches up from the bottom on each side of one cereal box with a ruler.

3. Trace a line all the way around the bottom of the box with your pencil.

4. Cut out the bottom of the box along the line with your scissors. Toss the rest of the cereal box into the recycle bin.

5. Using the grid on the back of the contact paper, cut out pieces that fit the outside and inside of the cereal box.

6. Peel off the back of the contact paper and stick it in place. Keep covering parts of the cereal box with contact paper until you have covered the whole thing.

7. Repeat steps 2 through 6 with the other four cereal boxes.

8. When your organizers are finished, line them up in a drawer to organize your stuff.

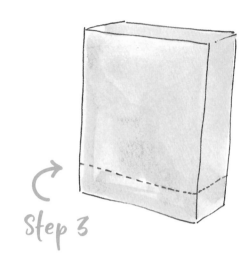

Step 3

Step 6

Finished!

42

PICTURE FRAME ERASABLE LIST MAKER

SKILL LEVEL

TIME

SUPPLIES

- [ ] picture frame with glass front
- [ ] white piece of paper
- [ ] pencil
- [ ] scissors
- [ ] dry erase marker

INSTRUCTIONS

looks good! ↘

1. Open the picture frame and remove the advertisement inside.

2. Place the advertisement insert on the white piece of paper and trace around it with a pencil.

3. Cut out the traced piece of paper.

4. Place inside the frame.

5. Your dry erase list maker is ready. Write on the glass with the dry erase marker and wipe off as needed.

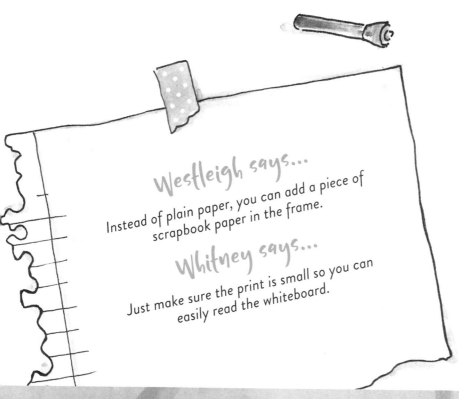

Westleigh says...

Instead of plain paper, you can add a piece of scrapbook paper in the frame.

Whitney says...

Just make sure the print is small so you can easily read the whiteboard.

43

CHALKBOARD LABEL STICKERS

SKILL LEVEL

TIME

SUPPLIES

- ☐ label template (make your own by tracing ours on page 140 and cutting it out)
- ☐ chalkboard contact paper
- ☐ scissors
- ☐ chalk

Westleigh says...

Chalkboard contact paper comes in different colors. I like pink the best.

Whitney says...

You can use our template or design your own labels. Try drawing one with a decorative border.

INSTRUCTIONS

1. Place the label template on the reverse side of the contact paper and trace around it.

2. Cut out the chalkboard label stickers with scissors.

3. Repeat steps 1 and 2 to create as many chalkboard label stickers as you like.

4. Stick the labels on notebooks, bins, pencil containers...whatever you'd like to label.

5. Prime the sticker by rubbing a layer of chalk on it and then erasing it.

6. Add the name you want to the label with chalk.

7. Your labels are ready to use to organize.

Step 1

Step 2

So cool!

44

Organizing Tip:

HOW TO FIND A PLACE FOR EVERYTHING

Whitney and Westleigh say...

We love to organize. Truly. Especially Westleigh. We love to open our drawers and see all our pencils and pens and note cards lined up. But really? It's so much easier to stay organized when you have a place for everything. We found this out early on when our bows used to get all tangled up in a big basket and they were so hard to find. That's the secret—creating a space for everything in your room. Do you need help figuring out where to put stuff? Here are some of our best tips.

1. Start with a drawer in your desk. Empty everything out of the drawer. Place the contents into three piles: the keep pile, the trash pile, and the donate pile. Place all the stuff to keep back into the drawer. (You can keep it organized with the craft on page 102.) Donate what needs to be donated and toss the rest. Repeat this process with all your drawers.

2. Organize your closet. Take everything out of your closet and repeat the same steps that you did with your desk drawer. Create a donate pile, a keep pile, and a trash pile for things that are too stained or damaged to donate. Then put the clothes you want to keep back into your closet. (We like to organize our closets by color.) Take the donate pile to the donation center and toss the rest.

3. Sometimes it's hard to find extra storage space in your room. We like to store stuff under our beds. Our mom got us some rolling storage boxes that open on one side. This is where we keep all our extra clothes that aren't in season and our extra blankets, pillows, and beach towels.

Staying organized is so much easier if you know where everything goes!

STUFF YOU CAN MAKE
TO ORGANIZE
Your Closet

45

PERSONALIZED CLOTHES HANGERS

SKILL LEVEL

TIME

SUPPLIES

- ☐ wood clothes hangers
- ☐ alphabet stickers
- ☐ library card
- ☐ ribbon

Westleigh says...

Our first and last names start with the same letter, so we chose a W.

Whitney says...

Instead of using stickers, you could buy a stencil (or print your own and cut it out) and stencil a letter onto the wood hangers.

INSTRUCTIONS

1. Wipe off the wood hangers with a cloth to make sure hangers are free of dust and dirt.

2. Find the sticker with the first letter of your first or last name.

3. Stick the letter onto the center of the hanger.

4. Press the edges of the sticker with a library card to make sure the sticker is completely stuck to the hanger.

5. Tie a ribbon around the top of the hanger and hang it up.

6. Repeat with as many hangers as you need for your closet.

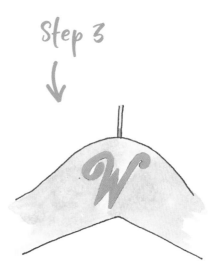

Step 3

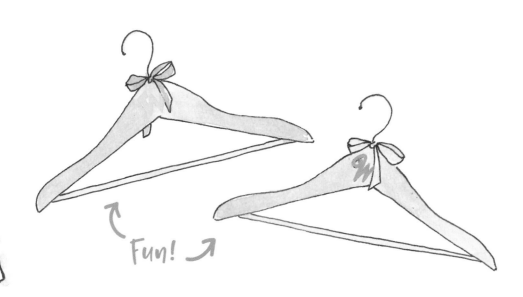

Fun!

46

BASKET TAG— YOU'RE IT!

SKILL LEVEL

TIME

SUPPLIES

- [ ] tag template (make your own by tracing ours on page 140 and cutting it out)
- [ ] scrapbook paper
- [ ] hole punch
- [ ] ribbon
- [ ] pencil
- [ ] markers
- [ ] white rectangle stickers

INSTRUCTIONS

1. Place the tag template on the back of the scrapbook paper and trace around it with your pencil.

2. Cut out the tag with scissors.

3. Place a white sticker in the center of the front of the tag.

4. Punch a hole in the corner of the tag.

5. Write whatever you want to organize on the tag.

6. Thread a ribbon through the hole in the corner and tie it onto a basket or tote.

7. Repeat steps 1 through 6 to create as many tags as you need.

8. Your tags are ready to organize your room.

Step 1

Step 4

Voila!

47

SIMPLE HAIR-TIE ORGANIZER

SKILL LEVEL

TIME

SUPPLIES

- ☐ 3 carabiner clips (you can find these at hardware or sporting goods stores)
- ☐ 3 hooks
- ☐ hair bands and hair ties

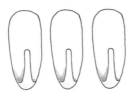

INSTRUCTIONS

1. Have a grown-up help you hang the hooks in your closet. You can hang them in a column (up and down) or a row (side by side).

2. Unclip the carabiner and place some hair ties or hair bands on it.

3. Clip the carabiner back in place and hang it on the hook.

4. Repeat the same process for the other two carabiners.

5. Next time you need a hair tie or band, they are all organized in one place.

Step 2 ⤷

Done! ↙

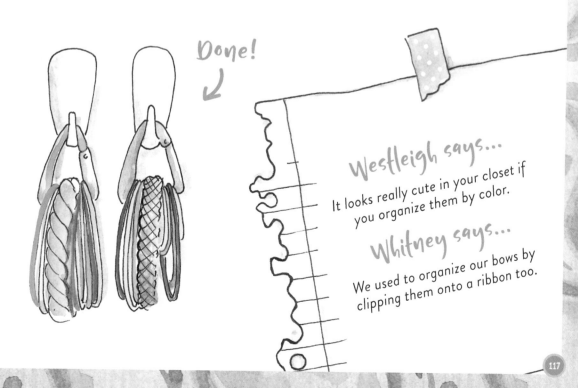

Westleigh says...

It looks really cute in your closet if you organize them by color.

Whitney says...

We used to organize our bows by clipping them onto a ribbon too.

48

Organizing Tip:
WHAT TO HANG AND WHAT TO FOLD

Whitney and Westleigh say...

Sometimes organizing your room is so much easier than it looks. We like to keep our stuff organized so we know where everything is in our room. The closet is the first place to start. If you need help organizing your closet, here are some tips on what to hang up on your new monogrammed hangers and what to fold and put away in your drawers:

1 Hang up dresses.

2 Hang up skirts (we like to hang two skirts to each clip hanger).

3 Hang up pants (we fold them over the hanger to hang).

4 Hang up hair ribbons and hair bandanas (we loop them over a hanger in the front of our closet).

5 Fold T-shirts.

6 Fold sweaters.

7 Fold jeans.

8 Fold shorts.

When you finish, step back and look at your closet. Is it smiling at you?
You are organized and ready to go.
Now go take on the day!

STUFF YOU CAN MAKE
TO DECORATE FOR THE
Holidays

49

XOXO PILLOW

SKILL LEVEL

TIME

SUPPLIES

- [ ] X and O stencils (make your own by tracing ours on page 141, or create one on a computer and print it out)
- [ ] white pillow cover with a zipper
- [ ] square piece of cardboard
- [ ] fabric marker
- [ ] pillow insert
- [ ] red felt
- [ ] fine-tipped white marker
- [ ] fabric glue

← Voilà!

INSTRUCTIONS

1. Spread out the white pillow cover on a table.

2. Place the piece of cardboard inside to protect the back from the glue.

3. Cut the X and O out of your stencils.

4. Place your X stencil on the felt. Trace inside the letter with a fabric marker.

5. Cut out the felt X.

6. Repeat steps 4 and 5 to create another X.

7. Place your O stencil on the felt. Trace inside the letter with a fabric marker.

8. Cut out the felt O.

9. Repeat steps 7 and 8 to create another O.

10. Place the Xs and Os on the white pillow cover. Position them the way you like them before you add glue.

11. After you are happy with your arrangement, glue the Xs and Os in place.

12. Let them dry.

13. Use the fine-tipped white marker to draw "stitches" around the edges of the letters on the pillow to make them look like they are sewed on.

14. Slip your XOXO cover over the pillow form.

Step 4

Step 11

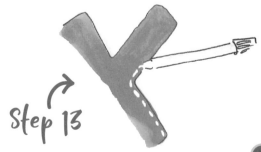

Step 13

50

EASTER RIBBON BASKET

SKILL LEVEL

TIME

SUPPLIES

- ☐ square basket
- ☐ polka-dot ribbon
- ☐ craft glue
- ☐ colorful buttons
- ☐ pencil
- ☐ scissors
- ☐ plastic Easter eggs

INSTRUCTIONS

1. Place the basket on a table.

2. Unroll the spool of ribbon and wrap it around the edge of the basket.

3. Mark with a pencil where the ribbon overlaps slightly around the basket.

4. Cut the piece of ribbon.

5. Add dots of craft glue around the edge of the basket.

6. Place the ribbon on the glue.

7. Let it dry.

8. With your pencil, mark the ribbon approximately every 4 inches.

9. Drop a dot of glue on your marks.

10. Place the buttons on the glue.

11. Let them dry.

12. Place Easter eggs in the basket in your room so your friends can discover them when they visit.

Step 2

Step 10

Done!

51

FALL BOOK-PAGE BANNER

SKILL LEVEL

TIME

SUPPLIES

- ☐ leaf templates of various sizes (make your own by tracing ours on page 142 and cutting them out)
- ☐ pages from a book you were going to recycle
- ☐ pencil
- ☐ scissors
- ☐ jute twine
- ☐ small clothespins
- ☐ ruler

INSTRUCTIONS

1. Place the leaves on the book pages. Trace around the leaves with a pencil.

2. Cut out the leaves.

3. Crinkle the leaf-shaped pages slightly.

4. Cut a piece of jute twine 36 inches long.

5. Using the small clothespins, clip the leaves onto the jute twine to make a banner.

6. Use the banner to decorate your room for fall.

Step 2

Step 3

Step 5

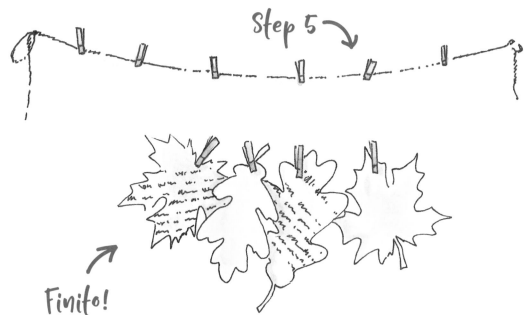

Finito!

52

CHRISTMAS TWIG WREATH

SKILL LEVEL

TIME

SUPPLIES

- [ ] white craft paint
- [ ] water
- [ ] bowl
- [ ] wax paper
- [ ] 100 small twigs from your yard
- [ ] 12-inch ring cut out of cardboard (you can also find round wreath forms at craft stores)
- [ ] glue

INSTRUCTIONS

1. Find 100 small twigs in the yard. Each twig should be no longer than 6 inches. The more forks in the twig, the better.

2. Pour a bottle of white craft paint into a bowl. Add 1 teaspoon of water and mix thoroughly.

3. Dip the twigs in the paint mixture.

4. Place the twigs on the wax paper to dry.

5. Continue dipping the twigs until all of them are painted.

6. Let them dry.

7. Glue one painted twig onto the cardboard (or wood) ring.

8. Glue the twigs in a clockwise direction until the entire ring is covered.

9. Wherever you can see parts of the cardboard, add a second layer of twigs.

10. Let the entire wreath dry.

11. Your wreath is ready to decorate for Christmas.

Step 2

Step 8

Beautiful!

Tutorials and Templates

HOW TO MAKE POM-POMS

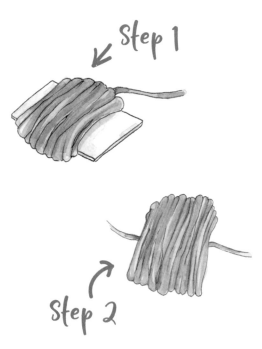

Step 1

Step 2

1. Start by wrapping yarn around a cardboard rectangle at least 45 times. The size of the piece of cardboard will determine the size of the pom-pom. And the more yarn you wrap around the cardboard, the thicker your pom-pom will be.

2. Gently slide the yarn off the cardboard and cut another piece of yarn approximately 10 inches long. Place your wrapped yarn on the 10-inch piece of yarn.

← Step 3

3 Tie the 10-inch piece of yarn around the center of your wrapped yarn. Tie it tightly and then tie it again. We don't want your pom-pom coming loose!

Step 4 →

4 Clip the loops of your pom-pom with scissors. Fluff the pom-pom and trim it until you have something that resembles a round pom-pom. (This is the fun part.) Be careful not to give it too much of a haircut, or your pom-pom will simply be a small pom instead!

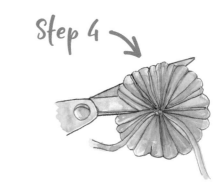

5 Repeat the steps until you have enough pom-poms for your project. Compare the pom-poms to each other as you make them to keep them all about the same size.

Pretty!

HOW TO MAKE TASSELS

1. Start by wrapping yarn around a cardboard rectangle at least 45 times. The size of the piece of cardboard will determine the size of the tassel. And the more yarn you wrap around the cardboard, the thicker your tassel will be.

Step 1

2. Cut two pieces of yarn approximately 10 inches long.

3. Thread one of the pieces between the loops of yarn and the cardboard and tie it off, leaving the strings hanging. This is the piece you will use to attach your tassel to something, such as a garland.

Step 3

4. Gently slide the loops of yarn off the cardboard.

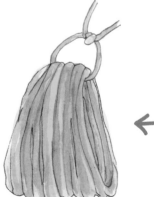

← Step 4

5 Tie the second 10-inch piece of yarn around the outside of your wrapped yarn, 1 inch from the top.

6 Tie it tightly, tie it again, and trim the ends.

7 Then simply clip the loops of your tassel with scissors.

8 Repeat the steps until you have enough tassels for your project. Compare the tassels to each other as you go to keep them all about the same size.

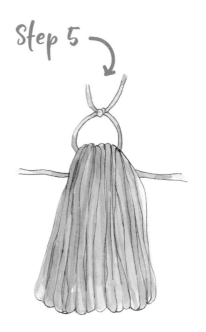

Step 5

Fabulous!

HOW TO USE MOD PODGE

Use Mod Podge to adhere one surface to another quickly and easily. It can be a little sticky. Literally. Here are some easy tips and tricks to using Mod Podge.

1. Use a sponge brush or a flat brush for easy application. Apply the Mod Podge to both pieces you are sticking together.

2. When applying Mod Podge to a surface, make sure you cover the area completely. This will prevent wrinkles. If you don't coat the entire surface with Mod Podge, the two pieces won't stick together properly.

3. Press the two pieces together. Use a roller on the top piece to prevent any bubbles from forming between them. The more time you take smoothing out the surface, the fewer bubbles you will have on your project.

4 Mod Podge dries quickly, so don't apply too much at one time, especially if you are working on a large surface. Each coat will dry in 15 to 20 minutes.

5 In addition to using like a glue, you can spread Mod Podge over your project to create a nice finish. Most projects need about two coats of Mod Podge. Make sure to let each coat dry thoroughly before you coat the next one.

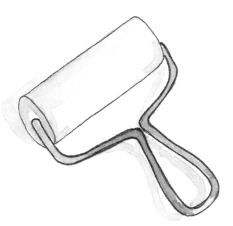

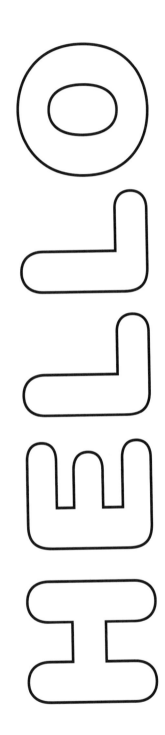

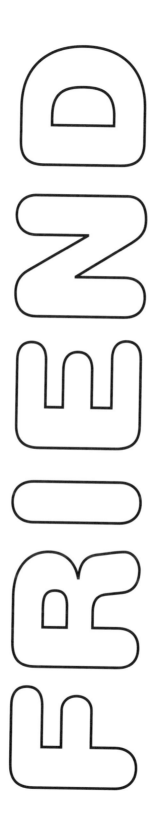

Flower

labels

leaves

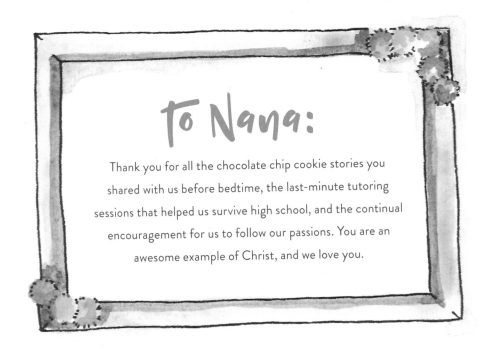

To Nana:

Thank you for all the chocolate chip cookie stories you shared with us before bedtime, the last-minute tutoring sessions that helped us survive high school, and the continual encouragement for us to follow our passions. You are an awesome example of Christ, and we love you.

Cover design by Nicole Dougherty

Interior design by Faceout Studio

Published in association with William K. Jensen Literary Agency, 119 Bampton Court, Eugene, Oregon 97404.

HARVEST KIDS is a trademark of The Hawkins Children's LLC. Harvest House Publishers, Inc., is the exclusive licensee of the trademark HARVEST KIDS.

DIY Room Makeover Ideas for Girls

Copyright © 2020 by KariAnne Wood, Whitney Wood, and Westleigh Wood

Artwork © 2020 by Michal Sparks

Published by Harvest House Publishers

Eugene, Oregon 97408

www.harvesthousepublishers.com

ISBN 978-0-7369-7412-7 (pbk.)

Library of Congress Cataloging-in-Publication Data is available at https://lccn.loc.gov/2019054614

Printed in China

20 21 22 23 24 25 26 27 28 / RDS-FO / 10 9 8 7 6 5 4 3 2 1